D0811822

OCEAN LIFE UP CLOSE

Manatees

by Rebecca Pettiford

BLASTOFF! READERS
3

Note to Librarians, Teachers, and Parents:

Blastoff! Readers are carefully developed by literacy experts and combine standards-based content with developmentally appropriate text.

Level 1 provides the most support through repetition of high-frequency words, light text, predictable sentence patterns, and strong visual support.

Level 2 offers early readers a bit more challenge through varied simple sentences, increased text load, and less repetition of high-frequency words.

Level 3 advances early-fluent readers toward fluency through increased text and concept load, less reliance on visuals, longer sentences, and more literary language.

Level 4 builds reading stamina by providing more text per page, increased use of punctuation, greater variation in sentence patterns, and increasingly challenging vocabulary.

Level 5 encourages children to move from "learning to read" to "reading to learn" by providing even more text, varied writing styles, and less familiar topics.

Whichever book is right for your reader, Blastoff! Readers are the perfect books to build confidence and encourage a love of reading that will last a lifetime!

This edition first published in 2017 by Bellwether Media, Inc.

No part of this publication may be reproduced in whole or in part without written permission of the publisher. For information regarding permission, write to Bellwether Media, Inc., Attention: Permissions Department, 5357 Penn Avenue South, Minneapolis, MN 55419.

Library of Congress Cataloging-in-Publication Data

Names: Pettiford, Rebecca, author.
Title: Manatees / by Rebecca Pettiford.
Description: Minneapolis, MN : Bellwether Media, Inc., 2017. | Series: Blastoff! Readers. Ocean Life Up Close | Includes bibliographical references and index. | Audience: Ages 5 to 8. | Audience: Grades K to 3.
Identifiers: LCCN 2016032045 (print) | LCCN 2016042926 (ebook) | ISBN 9781626175709 (hardcover : alk. paper) | ISBN 9781681032917 (ebook)
Subjects: LCSH: Manatees–Juvenile literature.
Classification: LCC QL737.S63 P48 2017 (print) | LCC QL737.S63 (ebook) | DDC 599.55–dc23
LC record available at https://lccn.loc.gov/2016032045

Editor: Christina Leighton   Designer: Brittany McIntosh
Printed in the United States of America, North Mankato, MN.

Table of Contents

What Are Manatees?

Manatees are large ocean **mammals**. They are often called sea cows.

They usually swim in shallow water. This lets them go to the surface quickly to breathe air.

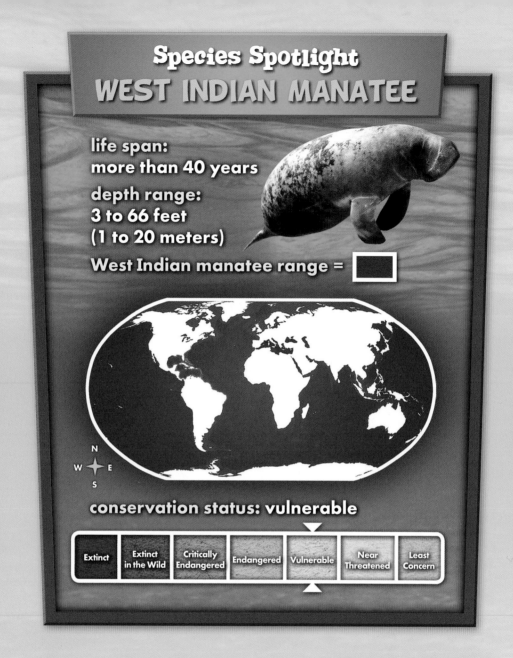

WEST INDIAN MANATEE

life span:
more than 40 years

depth range:
**3 to 66 feet
(1 to 20 meters)**

West Indian manatee range =

conservation status: vulnerable

Extinct	Extinct in the Wild	Critically Endangered	Endangered	Vulnerable	Near Threatened	Least Concern

There are three types of manatees. West Indian manatees swim along eastern North and South America.

Amazonian manatees live in the Amazon River. West African manatees live off Africa's western coast.

Amazonian manatee

Identify a Manatee

flat tail

whiskers

big lips

Manatees have whiskers and wrinkled faces. They have strong, flat tails that help them swim.

Their bodies have one **flipper** on each side. These help them turn. Sometimes, manatees use them to walk!

West Indian
manatee

Big and Slow

Manatees are slow swimmers. If they need to, they can swim 15 miles (24 kilometers) per hour.

West African manatee

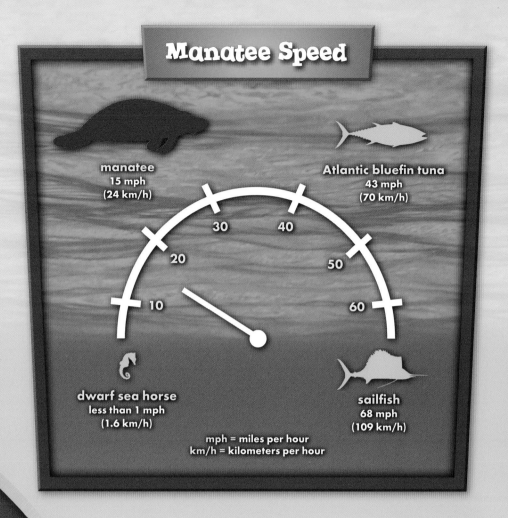

Manatee Speed

manatee
15 mph
(24 km/h)

Atlantic bluefin tuna
43 mph
(70 km/h)

30   40

20   50

10   60

dwarf sea horse
less than 1 mph
(1.6 km/h)

sailfish
68 mph
(109 km/h)

mph = miles per hour
km/h = kilometers per hour

Manatees do not have many **predators**. But humans have hurt their numbers. Laws are now in place to protect manatees.

Manatees have gray or grayish-brown bodies. They are between 8 and 13 feet (2.4 and 4 meters) long.

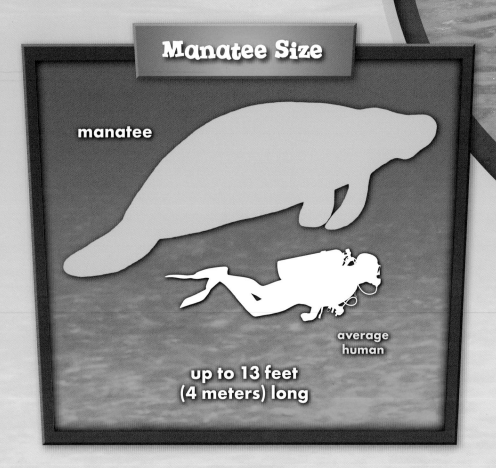

Manatee Size

manatee

average human

up to 13 feet (4 meters) long

They usually weigh between 440 and 1,300 pounds (200 and 590 kilograms)!

Plant Lovers

These **gentle** animals are **herbivores**. They eat sea grass and other **aquatic** plants.

Many manatees seek **freshwater** to drink. They are sometimes seen swimming up rivers.

Catch of the Day

turtle grass

manatee grass

water hyacinth

Manatees spend a lot of time alone. Sometimes they gather in **herds** to find food.

The herds also **migrate** when the water is too cold or low.

Manatee Calves

Mother manatees have one **calf** every two to three years.

Once it is born, a calf stays close
to its mother. It drinks her milk and
swims by her side.

Mothers whistle, squeak, or chirp
to their calves. They also teach
them where to find food, rest
areas, and warmer waters.

After about two years, the calves
are ready to swim on their own!

Glossary

aquatic—living in water

calf—a baby manatee

flipper—a flat, wide body part that is used for swimming

freshwater—water that is not salty

gentle—peaceful and good-natured

herbivores—animals that only eat plants

herds—groups of manatees

mammals—warm-blooded animals that have backbones and feed their young milk

migrate—to travel from one place to another, often with the seasons

predators—animals that hunt other animals for food

To Learn More

AT THE LIBRARY

Owen, Ruth. *Manatee Calves*. New York, N.Y.: Bearport, 2013.

Schuh, Mari. *Manatees*. Minneapolis, Minn.: Bullfrog Books, 2016.

Shea, Mary Molly. *Being a Manatee*. New York, N.Y.: Gareth Stevens Publishing, 2014.

ON THE WEB

Learning more about manatees is as easy as 1, 2, 3.

1. Go to www.factsurfer.com.

2. Enter "manatees" into the search box.

3. Click the "Surf" button and you will see a list of related web sites.

With factsurfer.com, finding more information is just a click away.

Index

The images in this book are reproduced through the courtesy of: Natalia Pryanishnikova/ Alamy, front cover; mpwoodib, pp. 3, 8 (bottom); Jeff Mondragon/ Age Fotostock/ SuperStock, pp. 4-5; Greg Amptman, p. 6; Doug Perrine/ Nature Picture Library, p. 7; Ethan Daniels, p. 8 (top left); gary powell, p. 8 (top center, top right); Wayne Lynch/ All Canada Photos/ SuperStock, p. 9; Tsuneo Nakamura/ Volvox Inc/ Alamy, p. 10; Bildagentur Zoonar GmbH, p. 13; James St. John/ Wikipedia, p. 15 (top left, top center); photoiconix, p. 15 (top right); Masa Ushioda/ Age Fotostock/ SuperStock, p. 15 (bottom); Alex Mustard/ Nature Picture Library, pp. 16-17; National Geographic Creative/ Alamy, p. 18; Norbert Probst/ imageBROKER/ SuperStock, p. 19; 33karen33, p. 20; NaturePL/ SuperStock, p. 21.